Still Life in N

Canvas of green, brushed with gold light,
Every detail sharp, a true delight.
Stillness captured in the artist's hand,
Nature's beauty on a timeless strand.

Rivers flowing like fine, soft silk,
Reflecting the sun, like a glass of milk.
This scene immortalized in our mind,
A masterpiece of life, pure and kind.

Where Time Stands Still

In the hush of twilight's glow,
Whispers of secrets softly flow.
Moments linger, shadows play,
Here in silence, time holds sway.

Stars awaken in the night,
Glistening points of purest light.
Hearts beat slowly, dreams unveiled,
In this realm, time has failed.

A river flows, yet stands so firm,
With every twist, the world can squirm.
Yet in space where stillness breathes,
Eternity weaves its gentle leaves.

Echoes of laughter gently ring,
Memories held in a fragile string.
Time, a friend, but also a thief,
In stillness, we find our belief.

In the heart of night, we dare to dream,
Chasing the stars' elusive gleam.
Where moments blend and time is nil,
We find our peace, where time stands still.

Unraveled Dreams

In the depths of night, they soar,
Wings of hope, they gently roar.
Threads of wishes, frayed and torn,
Unraveled dreams, in silence born.

Stars conspiring, thoughts take flight,
Painting shadows with pale light.
Hearts whisper secrets, old and new,
Seeking solace in midnight's hue.

Fragments of laughter, joy untamed,
In the canvas of night, they're framed.
Through tangled pathways, we will roam,
In every heartbeat, finding home.

Echoing wishes in the breeze,
As time unfolds with gentle ease.
Embers of hope flicker and gleam,
In the quiet, lay our dream.

With every step, the past unspools,
Through aching hearts and ancient rules.
Together we weave, with threads of light,
Unraveled dreams take endless flight.

Idyllic Respite

In fields where flowers sway,
Beneath the warm sun's ray,
Gentle breezes call me near,
A refuge, calm and clear.

The brook sings soft and low,
As winding waters flow,
Time slows its hurried pace,
In this serene embrace.

The sky wears hues of gold,
As stories of old unfold,
I breathe the fragrant air,
And find my worries rare.

The world outside may churn,
But here my heart can learn,
To cherish every beat,
Where nature and peace meet.

In moments that I steal,
With every light I feel,
Idyllic times like this,
Are treasures I won't miss.

Pockets of Peace

In corners of the day,
Where silence wants to play,
I find my hidden nooks,
Beyond the frantic books.

A cup of tea in hand,
The world feels so well-planned,
With whispers of the breeze,
And songs among the trees.

A simple path I tread,
Where worries drift like thread,
Each step a soft embrace,
In nature's gentle grace.

Clouds drift across the sky,
As time begins to fly,
In pockets where I dwell,
I find my heart's own spell.

Within this tranquil space,
I pause to find my place,
For in these pockets fair,
I breathe the fresher air.

Softly Falling Leaves

Autumn's breath, a sigh,
As leaves begin to fly,
They dance in crisp, cool air,
A vivid, golden flare.

Each leaf, a tale untold,
In colors rich and bold,
They carpet paths unseen,
In shades of bright maroon.

Whispers of the trees,
Carried on the breeze,
A gentle, calming sound,
As nature wraps around.

The sun begins to fade,
A soft, warm light cascades,
With every leaf that falls,
The quiet softly calls.

As twilight starts to show,
The stars begin to glow,
In this serene retreat,
Life's rhythm feels complete.

Whispered Promises of Dawn

Before the sun awakes,
When silence gently shakes,
The sky blushes with light,
As stars yield to the night.

A fragile morning glow,
Unfolds the world below,
With hues of softest peach,
New hopes that dawn can teach.

The dew-kissed blades arise,
Reflecting waking skies,
As shadows lose their hold,
In stories yet untold.

Birds sing a sweet refrain,
As joy breaks through the pain,
Each note, a promise shared,
Of moments that are bared.

In dawn's embrace I stand,
With dreams at my command,
For every gentle breath,
Reveals the strength in faith.

Dreams of a Forgotten Shore

Whispers of waves, soft and low,
Footprints fading, the tides bestow.
Seagulls cry as the sun descends,
In twilight's grasp, the ocean bends.

Shells tell secrets in the sand,
Echoes of laughter, hand in hand.
Lost in dreams where the sea meets sky,
Hearts adrift, time flowing by.

Moonlight dances on the crest,
In the shadows, souls find rest.
Memories linger, soft and sweet,
On this shore where dreamers meet.

The Promise of Tomorrow's Dawn

Stars fade quietly, making way,
For the bright hues of new day.
Hope is born with golden light,
As darkness gives in to the bright.

Birds sing melodies up high,
Awakening dreams that soar and fly.
Each moment holds a chance, anew,
In every heartbeat, hope shines through.

The path ahead may twist and turn,
But in our souls, bright flames will burn.
Embrace the dawn with open arms,
For the promise is in the charms.

Garden of Calm Reflections

In the heart of blooms so bright,
Whispers float in morning light.
Butterflies dance on gentle breeze,
In this haven, time seems to freeze.

Rippling waters mirror the sky,
As soft clouds drift gently by.
Petals fall in silent grace,
Nature's beauty, a warm embrace.

Each rustling leaf tells a tale,
Of peace found in this tranquil vale.
In quiet corners, solace grows,
In the garden where calm flows.

Waiting for the Sun to Sleep

The sky blushes with hues of gold,
As day's warm touch begins to fold.
Shadows lengthen, soft and deep,
In twilight's charm, the world does sleep.

Crisp air carries a gentle sigh,
As night unfolds its velvet sky.
Stars awaken, twinkling bright,
In this serene embrace of night.

Time stands still in this sweet pause,
Held in wonder, without cause.
For every sunset softly weeps,
A promise made, as daylight sleeps.

Echoes of Peaceful Retreat

In the hush of twilight's glow,
Whispers of the breezes blow.
Gentle rivers sing their song,
In this haven, we belong.

Nature cradles every sound,
As the heart finds common ground.
Softly echoes linger here,
Guiding spirits, drawing near.

Among the trees, the shadows play,
Painting night beneath the day.
Dancing leaves, a soothing art,
Quiet moments, soul and heart.

Fading light, the stars ignite,
Stars above, a wondrous sight.
In this space, our worries cease,
Finding comfort, love, and peace.

Finding Solace in Solitude

Amidst the silence, thoughts take flight,
In stillness blooms the mind's delight.
A whispered breeze in empty halls,
Echoes softly, gently calls.

Shadows stretch in softly lit,
Waves of calm in silence sit.
Breath of earth beneath my feet,
In this moment, life's complete.

Crickets sing the evening's tune,
Brightening the night's cool moon.
Stars like diamonds all aglow,
Guide us gently, lead us slow.

With each heartbeat, peace bestowed,
In this solitude, we've flowed.
Here in quiet, souls are free,
Finding solace, just to be.

The Harmony of Hidden Valley

In the valley where whispers sleep,
Nature's lullabies gently creep.
Mountains cradle the tender sky,
Boundless beauty, oh my, oh my!

Waterfalls cascade and spark,
Softly glistening in the dark.
Ferns and flowers whisper low,
Embracing secrets only they know.

Echoing songs of ages past,
In this valley, peace holds fast.
Within the blooms, life weaves anew,
In each petal, morning dew.

The dance of seasons, ever bright,
Colors blend in day and night.
Harmony in every breath,
In this retreat, there's no death.

Tides of Tranquil Waters

Waves caress the sandy shore,
Rhythms calling, evermore.
In the distance, seagulls soar,
Echoing dreams on the ocean floor.

Ripples kiss the gentle land,
Whispers held by nature's hand.
Soft horizons, blue and wide,
Where thoughts and waves collide.

Beneath the sun's warm embrace,
Time meanders at its pace.
Shells adorned with tales untold,
Bearing memories, ages old.

As the tide ebbs from its play,
Night descends on blushing bay.
Here in silence, hearts align,
In tranquil waters, we'll unwind.

Serenity in Shadows

In the stillness of the night,
Whispers dance in moonlight's glow.
Beneath the trees, cool and light,
Dreams unfold, soft and slow.

Silence weaves a gentle thread,
Binding hearts in tranquil grace.
In shadows, thoughts are quietly led,
To find solace in each space.

Echoes of a world unseen,
Flutter softly in the breeze.
As stars shimmer, calm and keen,
Connection deepens with such ease.

Here in the quiet hour's hold,
All worries seem to fade away.
In shadows, stories gently told,
Guide our souls until the day.

When dawn arrives with tender hue,
The shadows bow; they take their leave.
Yet in our hearts, we always knew,
Serenity is ours to weave.

The Quietude of Time

Time drips slowly from the sky,
Each moment lingers like a sigh.
In stillness, life begins to rhyme,
Finding peace in the quietude of time.

The clock's hands move with grace and care,
Painting shadows in golden air.
Each heartbeat shares a silent chime,
A melody of the quietude of time.

Ripples in a tranquil lake,
Whisper secrets; paths we take.
In every pause, a subtle climb,
Towards the essence of the quietude of time.

Clouds drift lazily, soft and shy,
Kissing horizons, low and high.
In their hush, we feel the prime,
Existence rests in the quietude of time.

As stars emerge in evening's sweep,
Their light a promise, soft and deep.
In this tapestry, we find our rhyme,
Living fully in the quietude of time.

Cradled by Darkness

In the arms of night so deep,
Secrets whisper, softly creep.
Wrapped in shadows, dreams take flight,
Cradled gently by the night.

Stars are candles in the sky,
Lighting paths for souls to fly.
In the stillness, fears take height,
Yet find comfort, cradled tight.

Moonlight spills like silken threads,
Weaving comfort where hope spreads.
In every darkness that ignites,
There is solace, cradled light.

Moments pause in velvet hours,
Nature's breath, the night restores.
Underneath the vast delights,
We find peace, cradled by nights.

So let the world outside be bold,
In our hearts, warmth we hold.
For in whispers, soft and slight,
We are cradled by the night.

Horizon's Breath

Where the sky meets land so vast,
Colors blend, shadows cast.
In this space, time feels so slow,
Horizon breathes, feelings flow.

Whispers of the ocean's tune,
Guide our hearts beneath the moon.
Each wave a promise, soft and low,
In the embrace of twilight's glow.

Birds fly high, tracing dreams,
Life unfolds in gentle streams.
Every sunset, golden show,
Tells us tales of hope and woe.

Mountains stand, firm in grace,
Holding memories in their space.
And as the world begins to slow,
Horizon sighs, whispers grow.

In every dawn that breaks anew,
We find strength from skies so blue.
With each breath, we come to know,
Life's vast beauty in horizon's flow.

Tranquil Echoes

In twilight's hush, the shadows play,
Whispers of night, call end of day.
Stars awaken, like dreams set free,
In tranquil echoes, souls find peace.

Moonlight dances, soft on the lake,
Ripples carry a gentle wake.
Nature's breath, a soothing song,
In tranquil echoes, all belong.

The breeze drifts slow, through silent trees,
Crickets sing, in harmonious ease.
Every heartbeat keeps perfect time,
In tranquil echoes, simple rhyme.

Clouds drift softly, in starlit skies,
Mirrors of calm, where stillness lies.
As dreams unfold, we rise and roam,
In tranquil echoes, we find home.

Whispering Earth

Beneath the sky, where grasses sway,
Whispers grow soft, in light of day.
Nature calls out, in colors bright,
Whispering earth, a pure delight.

Mountains stand tall, with secrets deep,
Roots intertwine, where silence weeps.
Every footprint tells a tale,
Whispering earth, where wonders hail.

Meadows alive, with violets' grace,
The wind's embrace, a gentle lace.
In every stone, and every leaf,
Whispering earth, a sacred belief.

Rivers hum tunes, as they flow wide,
Reflecting dreams, the world can't hide.
In nature's arms, we feel rebirth,
Whispering earth, our home of worth.

The Calm Before Dawn

A silent hush, the world awaits,
As shadows linger, night abates.
Stars blink slow, the sky turns blue,
The calm before dawn, a moment new.

Birds hold their breath, in quiet trees,
While dreams still float, upon the breeze.
A canvas waits, for colors bright,
The calm before dawn, gives birth to light.

The moon bows low, for sun's first ray,
In golden whispers, night gives way.
The horizon glows, a soft embrace,
The calm before dawn, a sacred space.

With every sigh, the night departs,
Hope unfolds, in tender hearts.
In stillness felt, a promise thrum,
The calm before dawn, a new day come.

Serenity's Embrace

In quiet corners of the mind,
Serenity waits, gently aligned.
Soft echoes hum, a soothing tune,
In serenity's embrace, all is strewn.

Morning dew on petals bright,
Glimmers softly in morning light.
Every breath, a calming flow,
In serenity's embrace, we grow.

Waves on the shore, a rhythmic dance,
Nature's heart, invites a chance.
With open arms, the world we face,
In serenity's embrace, find grace.

The sun dips low, in skies of gold,
As twilight whispers stories told.
In every moment, love's warm trace,
In serenity's embrace, find your place.

Shapes of Stillness

In the quiet, shadows play,
Softly drawn at close of day.
Whispers of the twilight sigh,
In the stillness, moments lie.

Leaves that dance without a sound,
Echoes of a peace profound.
Gentle ripples on the stream,
Time suspended, like a dream.

Muted colors blend and breathe,
Nature's calm, a gift to wreath.
Every form a tranquil song,
In this space, the heart belongs.

Silhouettes in twilight's glow,
Breath of night, a soft hello.
Each shape holds a story close,
In stillness, beauty interpose.

Softly now the dark unfolds,
Embraced by night, the silence holds.
In shapes of stillness, we find grace,
A gentle pause in time and space.

Fields of Solace

Vast horizons stretch anew,
In fields where gentle breezes blew.
Whispers tell of dreams untold,
In solace found, our hearts unfold.

Golden petals, kissed by light,
Softly sway in pure delight.
Each blade of grass, a tender touch,
In this place, we feel so much.

Over hills, the sun will soar,
As twilight beckons from the shore.
Shadows lengthen, softly blend,
In fields of solace, hearts ascend.

Every moment, sweetly shared,
In quiet corners, souls are bared.
Life's burdens slip away like dew,
In this field, we grow anew.

With every breath, joy does bloom,
In open skies, there's room for room.
Fields of solace cradle the heart,
Reminding us of nature's art.

A Restful Reverie

Within the hush of twilight's embrace,
Dreams cascade, a gentle pace.
Thoughts meander, softly drift,
In restful reverie, spirits lift.

Clouds adjusted to fading light,
Nights painted with stars so bright.
Every sigh, a peaceful ride,
In still reflection, we confide.

Moments linger, sweetly unwind,
In this space, what peace we find.
Worries fade like distant chime,
As dreams weave through the fabric of time.

Silken whispers, soft and clear,
Echo softly, drawing near.
In the calm, our souls ignite,
In restful reverie, pure delight.

Tonight we dance in shadows' glow,
Living echoes, ebb and flow.
In dreams we cast our hopes and fear,
In reverie, all things are near.

Beneath the Starlit Veil

Underneath the vast night sky,
Stars above, like dreams, they lie.
Twinkle softly, tales they weave,
Beneath the starlit veil, we believe.

Moonlight dances on the lake,
Whispers echo, hearts awake.
Every shadow, gently spun,
In this stillness, we are one.

Constellations, stories old,
Guide our thoughts, both brave and bold.
In their light, we find our way,
Beneath the starlit veil, we sway.

Moments captured in the dark,
Every heartbeat, every spark.
In this space, the world stands still,
Beneath the stars, we dream our fill.

So let us linger, night so fine,
In the glow, our spirits align.
With stars above and hearts so frail,
We find our truth beneath the veil.

Starry Solace

Under the blanket of night,
The stars whisper dreams bright.
Each twinkle, a warm embrace,
Guiding us to a safe space.

The moon casts a silver gleam,
Filling hearts with a soft beam.
In silence, worries take flight,
Lost in the vastness of night.

Soft breezes dance with the trees,
Carrying secrets on the breeze.
Nature hums a gentle tune,
Cradled beneath the watchful moon.

In moments of quiet and peace,
All burdens begin to cease.
Together in this starlit haze,
We find comfort in the maze.

So here beneath the night's shroud,
We share dreams and laugh out loud.
With every star overhead,
Our spirits are gently led.

Gathering Clouds of Comfort

Gray clouds gather high above,
Whispering secrets, gentle, love.
They promise rain, a sweet release,
Wrapping the world in soft peace.

The wind hums with a soothing song,
As nature's chorus sings along.
Each drop will kiss the thirsty ground,
In their embrace, warmth is found.

A palette of grays and blues,
Witness to life's vibrant hues.
Together, the clouds softly drift,
Bestowing on us a lovely gift.

With every patter, heartbeats slow,
As we feel the soothing flow.
The world wrapped in a watery quilt,
A tranquil calm, no need for guilt.

Embraced by the tempest's grace,
We find comfort in this space.
In gathering clouds, we truly see,
Life's beauty in simplicity.

The Comforting Stillness

In quiet moments we retreat,
To the solace of stillness, sweet.
A breath held in the tranquil air,
Where worries fade, light as a prayer.

The world outside may whirl and spin,
But here is where our peace begins.
Gentle whispers brush the ear,
In the calm, all shadows clear.

Like a soft blanket, time suspends,
Each heartbeat a hymn that mends.
Thoughts drift like leaves on a stream,
In stillness, we cradle our dream.

The sun dips low, a glorious sight,
Wrapping us in its warm light.
With every silence, we align,
Finding strength in the divine.

So let this stillness be our guide,
As it wraps us, deep inside.
In corners quiet, spirits soar,
Finding comfort forevermore.

The Art of Rest

In the garden, soft and wide,
Nature holds us, arms open wide.
With petals bright and skies so blue,
We find the art of resting true.

Laying down all cares of the day,
In the breeze, worries drift away.
Each daisy nods in the gentle sun,
An invitation for everyone.

The rustling leaves, a soft caress,
Whispers of peace that gently press.
Each moment swells, inviting grace,
A sweet comfort in this place.

Clouds drift lazily, no need to race,
Time unfolds at its own pace.
In stillness, we gather our thoughts,
Finding solace in life's simple knots.

The art of rest, a cherished gift,
In each quiet breath, our spirits lift.
So with open hearts, we truly see,
The beauty of calm, forever free.

The Beauty of Paused Motion

In stillness, time takes breath,
A quiet dance, a whispered waltz,
Leaves sway gently, holding death,
While shadows stretch, the world exalts.

Moments linger, soft embrace,
A heartbeat echoes in the void,
Life's quicksilver finds its place,
In every pause, stories deployed.

Ice crystals form on midnight's edge,
As stars play hide and seek with night,
The universe forms a solemn pledge,
To cradle each flicker of light.

What if silence held the key?
Each heartbeat counts like grains of sand,
In the beauty of 'let it be,'
A symphony of fate, so grand.

Each breath a circle, a gentle spin,
In motion's grasp, we find reprieve,
For in the still, we learn to win,
The hidden gems that we believe.

Dreams Under a Velvet Sky

Underneath the vast expanse,
Stars like whispers, softly gleam,
Moonlight casts a timeless glance,
Awakening the heart to dream.

A tapestry of night unfolds,
Stories written in silken thread,
In shadows deep, a secret holds,
The echoes of the dreams we've bred.

Waves of starlight brush the soul,
In cosmic waves, we drift alight,
With each breath, we seek the whole,
In slumber's grasp, we touch the night.

The quiet hum of nightingale,
Guides our wishes to the stars,
In the dark, our spirits sail,
Embracing freedom, we break bars.

So let the velvet skies inspire,
Awake the dreams that time has sewn,
In the light of midnight's fire,
We find the magic, we have known.

In the Arms of Hushed Moments

Time slows down in gentle grace,
As moments wrap like velvet lace,
In quiet corners, silence sings,
Embracing all the joy it brings.

A breath between the chaos reigns,
Where stillness speaks without constraints,
Whispers echo in quiet halls,
In these arms, the world enthralls.

The clocks will pause, the heart will sway,
In hushed embrace, we drift away,
To find a peace in every thought,
In stillness, life is gently caught.

Every heartbeat's a soft refrain,
A song composed of joy and pain,
In these moments, truth resides,
Where serenity abides and hides.

So hug the quiet, hold it tight,
In the soft glow of fading light,
For in these arms, we find our way,
To cherish every fragile day.

Soft Footsteps of Twilight

As daylight wanes, shadows conspire,
Their soft embrace ignites the sky,
Footsteps whisper, as dreams conspire,
In twilight's glow, we learn to fly.

An orchestra of fading light,
Nature sighs in purples and golds,
In this hush, the world feels right,
As secrets of the night unfold.

Each step a dance on dewy grass,
The breeze carries tales of yore,
In this moment, all things pass,
Yet promise lingers at the door.

Night blossoms forth, the stars ascend,
Crescendo of the night's embrace,
In twilight's arms, our hearts will blend,
With all that's lost, we find our place.

So walk with me through dusky dreams,
Where time suspends, and hope redeems,
In soft footsteps, together glide,
Through twilight's veil, we shall abide.

The End of the Day

As the sun sinks low, shadows creep,
Whispers of twilight, calm and deep.
Colors blend in a soft embrace,
Nature sighs in this sacred space.

Stars begin to flicker and gleam,
Casting thoughts like a gentle dream.
The world exhales, in silence, stays,
In the serene end of the day.

Moonlight dances on the still lake,
Ripples whisper what dreams may wake.
A moment captured, time stands still,
Hearts are softened by evening's chill.

Birds retreat to their cozy nests,
As the sky dons its velvet vests.
The breeze carries a sweet refrain,
A lullaby for night's gentle reign.

With each minute, the world unwinds,
In the quiet, solace one finds.
As darkness falls, peace holds sway,
Embracing the end of the day.

Fading Footsteps

Along the path where memories bloom,
Echoes linger, dispelling gloom.
Each step taken, a story told,
Fading softly as time grows old.

Leaves rustle in the autumn breeze,
Carrying whispers through the trees.
Footprints vanish in the soft ground,
Silent stories yet to be found.

The past lingers in dusky light,
Fleeting shadows that feel so right.
With every dawn, we move along,
Yet in our hearts, they still belong.

Through winding roads and endless skies,
The journey flows as the river flies.
Each moment cherished, a fleeting guest,
Yet in the soul, they find their rest.

So let us wander, hand in hand,
Through the meadows, across the sand.
For in the fading, they remain,
Footsteps echoing, love's sweet gain.

Reflective Meadows

In the morning's golden hue,
Meadows stretch, adorned with dew.
Gentle whispers of the breeze,
Nature hums with tranquil ease.

Flowers bloom in vibrant light,
A canvas painted pure and bright.
Every color tells a tale,
Of soft winds and gentle gales.

Beside the stream, reflections play,
Mirroring dreams of yesterday.
Time slows down in this embrace,
Lost in nature's tender grace.

Clouds drift lazily overhead,
While thoughts like petals gently spread.
In this haven, worries cease,
Here, the heart can find its peace.

As daylight wanes, stars take flight,
The meadow glows softly at night.
In dreams, we wander, souls set free,
In reflective meadows, just you and me.

Secrets of the Silent Forest

In the heart where whispers dwell,
Secrets hidden, a timeless spell.
Tall trees stand as ancient guards,
Holding stories, etched in shards.

Sunlight filters through the leaves,
Dancing gently, the spirit weaves.
Each rustle tells of lives unseen,
In shadows deep, where few have been.

Footsteps light on a carpeted floor,
Soft as dreams, opening doors.
The forest breathes, a soothing balm,
Inviting seekers to find their calm.

With every glance, a tale unfolds,
Of woodland creatures, brave and bold.
The silence sings in nature's way,
Guiding lost souls who wander astray.

As twilight beckons, the night draws near,
The forest stirs, whispers clear.
In this haven of peace and rest,
The silent forest holds its chest.

The Gentle Causation of Sleep

In twilight's soft embrace we drift,
Whispers of night begin to lift,
Dreams unfurl on golden seams,
Resting deep in silent themes.

Moonlight dances on the floor,
Shadows stretch, then fade once more,
A lullaby of stars above,
Filling hearts with gentle love.

Time slows down, the world grows dim,
Each breath a hymn, a sacred whim,
Wrapped in warmth, we find our place,
In the stillness, we leave no trace.

Gentle sighs and tender thoughts,
Floating free, where worries rot,
Nestled close, we softly sway,
In the arms of night, we lay.

As dawn approaches, dreams retreat,
Holding fast to the quiet beat,
Sleep's sweet call, a soft goodbye,
In morning's glow, our spirits fly.

Veils of Mist and Quietude

In morning's breath, the mists unfold,
A world transformed, serene and bold,
Veils of gray dance in the air,
Whispers of peace, a gentle prayer.

Through silver shrouds, the shadows creep,
Nature's secret, vast and deep,
A tranquil bond, the heart's soft sigh,
In quietude, the soul can fly.

The brook sings low, a lullaby,
Among the trees, its whispers lie,
Leaves like mirrors, reflecting grace,
In this haven, we find our place.

Each step we take, the stillness grows,
With every breath, a calm bestows,
In the mist, life's burdens fade,
Lost in thoughts, where dreams are laid.

As daylight breaks, the veils dispel,
Yet in our hearts, we still can dwell,
For in the quiet, peace ignites,
Forever cherished, our spirit lights.

Rays of Hope in Still Waters

In the depths, reflections gleam,
Whispers echo like a dream,
Softly shining, hope appears,
Washing away the veils of fears.

Ripples spread, a tender sigh,
As sunlight dances, aiming high,
In the stillness, hearts unite,
Filled with warmth, dispelling night.

Beneath the surface, truth runs clear,
In gentle waves, our dreams draw near,
Every pulse a promise made,
In stillness, all doubts slowly fade.

The water cradles every wish,
A serene bond, a tranquil bliss,
In fleeting moments, joy takes flight,
Carried softly by the light.

As shadows part, the dawn unfolds,
Embracing hope with arms of gold,
In still waters, we find the key,
To cherish life, and simply be.

Chasing Shadows of the Past

In quiet halls where echoes play,
Shadows linger, fade away,
Each footstep tells a tale once known,
While memories weave in whispers grown.

Through twisted paths of time and space,
We chase the ghosts of lost embrace,
Each fleeting shadow, a glance we take,
In fading light, the heart can break.

Yet in the dusk, a truth remains,
In every joy, in all the pains,
Buried deep, a spark ignites,
Guiding us through endless nights.

As twilight falls, we look behind,
Finding strength in the ties that bind,
Shadows dance, our past's refrain,
A bittersweet, yet sweetened gain.

In chasing shadows, we reclaim,
The stories carved, the love's true name,
For in the dusk, we come to see,
That every shadow sets us free.

Serenity in Shadows

In twilight's hush, where whispers dwell,
Soft shadows creep, a comforting spell.
The moonlight dances on silent streams,
Embracing secrets in silver beams.

A gentle breeze through lingering trees,
Carries the tales of forgotten ease.
Each rustle sings of a moment lost,
In nature's arms, we find our cost.

The world fades dim, with colors muted,
Beneath the stars, our hearts are rooted.
A stillness wraps the trembling night,
As dreams unfurl in the soft twilight.

In shadows deep, we pause and find,
The beauty cloaked in the night unblind.
Here in this void, peace takes its claim,
Serenity whispers, and calls our name.

Cradled by the Earth

Upon the ground where wildflowers grow,
In dampened soil, life finds its flow.
The warmth of sun, the cool of shade,
Nature's cradle, where dreams are laid.

Rivers run deep, weaving through land,
Each twist and turn, a guiding hand.
Mountains stand tall, guardians of grace,
Holding the stories of time and space.

In autumn's chill, leaves dance and fall,
Whispering secrets, answering the call.
Bare feet touch earth, we're grounded here,
In the embrace of nature, crystal clear.

The wind hums softly, a calming song,
Echoing rhythms where we belong.
Cradled by the earth, we learn to trust,
In every moment, it's pure and just.

Embracing Stillness

In the silence vast, we find our peace,
A gentle pause, where worries cease.
The ticking clock fades to quiet hum,
In stillness bred, we come undone.

Here in the calm, voices recede,
Echoing thoughts, planting the seed.
A breath, a moment, a chance to reflect,
In the hush of time, we connect.

The heart beats slow, a rhythmic flow,
Finding the grace in the ebb and glow.
In every sigh, the world retreats,
Embracing stillness, our spirit meets.

With open arms, we welcome the now,
In tranquil waters, we learn to bow.
The richness of quiet, our souls awaken,
In this stillness shared, we are unshaken.

A World Unseen

Beneath our feet, a magic brews,
In shadows cast, life quietly moves.
Eyes closed tight, we sense the spark,
In every heartbeat, the unseen arc.

The dance of dust, in sunlit rays,
A fleeting glimpse of hidden ways.
While world rushes on, we stand and pause,
In whispered wonders, we find our cause.

Between the lines of what we know,
A world unfolds, like rivers flow.
The uncharted paths call us to stray,
In depths of silence, the heart will play.

With open minds, we gaze within,
Where reality fades, dreams begin.
In every moment, explore the keen,
And dance through life in a world unseen.

Emptied Spaces

In corners where shadows linger,
Whispers fade into the night,
Echoes of a time now gone,
Lone memories take flight.

Dust settles on forgotten dreams,
Each breath feels just a sigh,
Spaces once filled with laughter,
Now only silence replies.

Walls that held our secrets tight,
Now stand in solemn grace,
Time moves on, yet still, we yearn,
For warmth in empty space.

We gather the remnants of joy,
To light the darkened room,
In the stillness, truth remains,
Blooming from silent gloom.

Yet in these emptied chambers,
Hearts still beat with fierce desire,
For bridges of love to bind us,
Through the ashes, we aspire.

Full Hearts

In laughter shared and secrets told,
Our spirits dance like flames,
A bond so strong, a treasure bright,
Together we cast names.

Through trials faced and storms endured,
We stand, unbreakable, whole,
With every heartbeat, we create,
A symphony of soul.

Each moment filled with vibrant life,
Reflects in every glance,
With open arms and laughter's gift,
We leap, we take a chance.

Full hearts embrace the sunlit paths,
In colors bold and true,
Side by side, our spirits soar,
In all we dare to do.

As seasons change and years roll on,
We'll weave our stories tight,
In every chapter, we'll find peace,
That lasts beyond the night.

Beneath the Blanket of Silence

Beneath the stars, a hush descends,
Whispers held in stillness,
A world wrapped in velvet calm,
Embracing the night's chillness.

The moon weaves tales of ancient dreams,
As shadows drift and sigh,
In this serene, enchanted space,
Time seems to gently fly.

Each breath a note in silence played,
A melody so pure,
Cradled by the night's embrace,
In darkness, we endure.

Thoughts wandering like wandering stars,
Through realms we cannot see,
In the quiet of this moment,
We find who we can be.

So let us linger here awhile,
Beneath this tender sky,
For in the folds of silence deep,
Our souls can learn to fly.

A Tapestry Woven in Calm

Threads of gold and azure weave,
A tapestry unfolds,
In patterns soft, where dreams reside,
And mysteries are told.

Each stitch a moment captured,
In colors rich and bright,
Together forming memories,
That dance in pure delight.

With every knot, a story grows,
Of laughter, love, and pain,
In this grand design of life,
Soft joy and quiet rain.

Woven with the hands of time,
Beneath the watchful stars,
Our hearts entwined in radiant hues,
Like light that travels far.

So let the loom spin on and on,
In gentle grace, we'll find,
A world adorned with vibrant threads,
A peace so intertwined.

The Last Light of Evening

As daylight slips beyond the hills,
The horizon blushes gold,
A gentle sigh, the day concedes,
As twilight's arms unfold.

Shadows stretch and colors blend,
A canvas rich and deep,
In every hue, a story waits,
As nature climbs to sleep.

The whispers of the evening breeze,
Soft secrets softly blown,
In the quiet, we find solace,
In the shadows we are grown.

Last light dances on the leaves,
A fleeting, tender grace,
Embracing all that has been lived,
In this sacred space.

So let us cherish every glow,
That evening's light may bring,
For in the dark, a promise lies,
Of hope, in stillness, sing.

Nature's Quiet Symphony

In the forest where whispers play,
Trees sway gently, night and day.
Birds sing softly, a heartfelt tune,
Nature's orchestra beneath the moon.

Waves crash lightly against the shore,
Crickets chirp, a sweet encore.
Leaves rustle in the cool night air,
Harmony found everywhere.

Mountains stand tall, their echoes call,
The world is still, yet feels so small.
Stars twinkle bright in the velvet sky,
A symphony sung by the earth, oh my!

Rivers flow with a melodic grace,
Reflecting light, a sacred space.
Life's whispers blend in nature's song,
A symphony of peace all along.

In this quiet, we find our rest,
Nature's beauty, truly blessed.
As night drapes the world in its hush,
We nurture dreams amidst the rush.

Reflections in Still Waters

Beneath the sky, a mirror lies,
Reflecting dreams and whispered sighs.
Ripples dance with each gentle breeze,
Nature's canvas, a moment to seize.

The trees lean in to catch a glance,
Water's stillness, a tranquil dance.
Moonbeams kiss the glassy sheen,
Painting shadows, soft and serene.

Frogs croak softly from the edge,
Sharing secrets from their hedge.
Fish dart through the depths below,
In still waters, peace starts to flow.

A feather floats, a fleeting gift,
Capturing time in nature's drift.
Each reflection tells a story true,
Of simple joys that we pursue.

As evening falls, the stars appear,
In still waters, dreams draw near.
Life pauses in this sacred space,
Where troubles fade, leaving only grace.

Resting Leaves and Moonlight

Underneath the ancient trees,
Leaves whisper softly with the breeze.
Moonlight dances on the ground,
In this silence, peace is found.

Branches cradle the night so tight,
Embracing shadows, soft and light.
Resting leaves, a golden hue,
Drifting dreams, old yet new.

The air is filled with a gentle hush,
As nature pauses, a calming rush.
Every spark and every glow,
Breathes life into the world below.

Crickets serenade the night,
Stars join in, a joyful light.
In this magic, time stands still,
As waves of calmness slowly thrill.

Resting leaves beneath the moon,
Whispers of night, a soothing tune.
In the stillness, we find our place,
Embraced by nature's warm embrace.

Lanterns of Peace

In the dusk, where shadows play,
Lanterns flicker, guiding the way.
Each glowing light, a story untold,
A beacon of hope, shining bold.

Like stars fallen from the sky,
Their warmth soothes, and spirits fly.
Paths illuminated, hearts set free,
Lanterns of peace for you and me.

In gardens lush, they sway and dance,
Inviting all to take a chance.
Rekindle dreams, rekindle light,
In the embrace of the gentle night.

With every flame, worries fade,
A tranquil heart, like a serenade.
Together we walk this peaceful road,
Carrying the light, sharing the load.

As lanterns glow beneath the trees,
We find our rest, we find our ease.
In the night, we rise above,
Harnessing the power of love.

Silent Echoes of Dusk

Whispers float on evening's breath,
Shadows dance where light meets death.
Stars awaken, soft and bright,
Cradling dreams in velvet night.

The moon casts down its silver gaze,
While twilight stirs in tender ways.
Old memories begin to stir,
In the stillness, thoughts confer.

Gentle winds hum lullabies,
Pulling whispers from the skies.
As daylight fades, our worries rest,
In dusk's embrace, we feel the best.

With every heartbeat, silence grows,
In twilight's weave, the magic flows.
Each echo hold a tale untold,
In the hush, our hearts unfold.

Let the night wrap us in peace,
As chaos fades, our minds release.
In silent echoes, we find grace,
A tranquil moment, a sacred space.

Tranquility's Embrace

Softly, the dawn greets the earth,
In gentle light, there is rebirth.
Nature whispers, calm and clear,
In tranquility, we find no fear.

The river flows with steady grace,
Holding secrets in its embrace.
Birds take flight in azure skies,
While silence lingers, softly sighs.

In every leaf, a story sings,
A peaceful heart, to hope it clings.
Amidst the chaos, stillness reigns,
In tranquility, love remains.

Each wave that crashes finds its way,
To soothe the soul at close of day.
In quiet moments, we discover,
The beauty found in one another.

Let us unearth this sacred space,
Where every heartbeat finds its place.
Embraced by stillness, we arise,
With hope and peace beneath the skies.

The Stillness Between Heartbeats

In the silence, a heartbeat waits,
Suspended time, at destiny's gates.
Moments linger, breaths align,
In the stillness, our souls entwine.

Between each tick, a world unfolds,
Stories whispered, secrets told.
In absence of sound, we find the core,
Of love's abundance, and so much more.

A fleeting pause, where hopes ignite,
Dreams are born in the soft twilight.
Each beat a promise, a soft caress,
In the stillness lies our happiness.

Beneath the stars, we share this space,
The pauses shaped in time's embrace.
Stillness holds what words can't share,
In every heartbeat, we find what's rare.

Together, we dance in silence deep,
Where the heart's soft whispers never sleep.
In moments brief, a truth we keep,
A love that wakes, a dream to leap.

Moments of Gentle Surrender

In twilight's hug, we let it go,
Each burden light, each worry slow.
The world fades softly, in true release,
A moment's grace, a heart at peace.

Clouds drift gently across the sky,
Carrying dreams that soar and fly.
With every sigh, we shed our weight,
In surrender, we embrace fate.

Let silence wrap us, hold us near,
In the stillness, we find what's dear.
Time slows down, each breath a prayer,
In moments soft, we find our care.

Beneath the stars, we learn to trust,
In gentle waves of cosmic dust.
Embracing change with open hearts,
A dance of souls, where beauty starts.

Awake in stillness, we fear no more,
As moments pass, we learn to soar.
In gentle surrender, we find our way,
To love and light at the close of day.

Quietude of the Heart

In the stillness, shadows play,
Softly guiding night and day.
A whisper held in silent breath,
Where peace flourishes, free from death.

Gentle thoughts begin to weave,
In the tranquil scenes we believe.
A sigh escapes, a gentle start,
Embracing the quietude of the heart.

Stars above with gentle gleam,
Filling spaces, like a dream.
Moonlit dances on the floor,
Calm reflections, evermore.

Time stands still, a soft embrace,
In this sacred, cherished space.
Here we linger, sensing light,
Quietude enfolds the night.

As dawn unfolds with hues anew,
Hope and love will see us through.
In every heartbeat, peace we find,
Quietude, the soul's aligned.

Tranquil Whispers

Where rivers flow with whispered dreams,
A soft serenade, or so it seems.
Nature sings a lullaby,
Underneath the vast, blue sky.

Leaves rustle gently in the breeze,
Carrying secrets, aiming to please.
In this stillness, magic grows,
Amongst the trees, where silence flows.

Morning light begins to crest,
Inviting all to take a rest.
Harmony in every sound,
In tranquil whispers all around.

Colors paint the world anew,
With each moment, hope breaks through.
Softly calls the heart's delight,
In the calm of peaceful night.

So let us find that sacred space,
In tranquil whispers, feel the grace.
With every breath, we learn to see,
A world wrapped in serenity.

The Sigh of Nature

In twilight hours, the world exhales,
Nature speaks through gentle gales.
Mountains stand in silent grace,
Cradling life in their embrace.

Streams caress the waiting shore,
Inviting all to seek for more.
Softened echoes fill the air,
The sigh of nature, pure and rare.

Clouds drift lazily, shadows cast,
Whispers of time, shadowed past.
In every rustle, every call,
Nature sighs and binds us all.

Birds alight on branches high,
Carved against the deep, blue sky.
With every flutter, life anew,
The sigh of nature, drifting through.

So listen close, be still, be free,
For nature's heart beats endlessly.
In its rhythm, wisdom flows,
The sigh of nature, always knows.

Gentle Stirrings

At dawn, the world begins to wake,
With gentle stirrings, dreams will break.
Morning light paints every hue,
Soft caress, a day anew.

Birdsongs weave through emerald leaves,
Nature dances, weaves and breathes.
In quiet moments, hearts do yearn,
For gentle stirrings, to discern.

Sunbeams kiss the waking ground,
In every corner, life is found.
A breath of hope, the morning's cheer,
With gentle stirrings, we draw near.

The quiet rustle of the grass,
As shadows stretch and moments pass.
In every heartbeat, joy will bloom,
In gentle stirrings, dispel the gloom.

So take a moment, pause and feel,
The gentle stirrings that reveal.
A symphony of life's sweet song,
In twilight's promise, we belong.

The Sweetness of Slumber

In the quiet night so deep,
Dreams descend as one falls asleep.
Whispers of stars gently twine,
Wrapped in a fog of serene divine.

Crickets sing a lullaby near,
Each note soft, delicate, and clear.
Moonlight dances on silken sheets,
Where the heart and the stillness meets.

Ember glow of the fireplace bright,
Shadows play in the soft moonlight.
Time drifts away, wrapped in a haze,
Nostalgic echoes, heart's gentle praise.

In this moment, the world feels right,
Held in the arms of the endless night.
Peace flows in like a gentle stream,
Life unfolds in a tender dream.

Awakened softly by dawn's sweet kiss,
With every ray, there's a feeling of bliss.
The sweetness of slumber, a treasure we keep,
In the quiet retreat, we cherish our sleep.

Stillness in Bloom

In gardens where silence whispers low,
Petals soft in a gentle flow.
The fragrance dances in the breeze,
Nature's hymn, a tranquil tease.

Amidst the blooms, time stands still,
A moment captured, a heart to fill.
Colors brush against the day,
Infinite beauty, in soft array.

Butterflies flutter, kiss the air,
In this stillness, nothing's rare.
Life blossoming without a sound,
Whispers of joy where peace is found.

Every leaf tells a story anew,
Of seasons past and skies so blue.
In the quiet, a symphony plays,
Eternal dance in nature's gaze.

As day gives way to soft twilight,
Stars emerge in the gentle night.
Stillness lingers, secrets loom,
In the heart of nature's bloom.

Echoing Calm

In the depths of the forest's embrace,
Silence reigns in a sacred space.
Leaves rustle in whispers soft,
Echoing calm as the senses waft.

Waves of peace gently unfold,
Footsteps muted, stories untold.
Crickets chirp a rhythmic beat,
Nature's echo, a heart's retreat.

Sky stretches wide, painted in blue,
Clouds drift lazily, a calming hue.
With each breath, the soul unwinds,
Tranquility found in nature's finds.

Ripples on water, a mirror's grace,
Reflecting stillness, a tranquil face.
Time pauses softly, a tender sigh,
In echoes of calm, the heart learns to fly.

As shadows lengthen, twilight glows,
A gentle hush where the river flows.
In every silence, the spirit gleams,
Finding the peace within our dreams.

Touching Tranquility

In the quiet hour before the dawn,
A serene hush drapes the lawn.
Nature breathes in gentle grace,
Touching tranquility, a sacred space.

Birds begin their morning song,
Notes of joy where they belong.
Sunrise spills its golden light,
Painting the world in hues so bright.

The breeze carries stories untold,
Of love and life, of brave and bold.
In every petal, in every leaf,
Touching tranquility, a sweet relief.

Morning's blush on the flower's face,
In its beauty, a warm embrace.
Hearts open up to the new day's call,
Finding peace, embracing it all.

As the day unfolds, hope takes flight,
In every moment, pure delight.
Touching tranquility, a gentle balm,
In nature's rhythm, we find our calm.

Slumbering Landscapes

Gentle hills in evening light,
Rolling dreams with fading sight,
Whispers soft across the land,
Night's embrace, a tender hand.

Mountains cradle stars so bright,
In the calm of velvet night,
Rivers hum a lullaby,
As the moon begins to fly.

Fields of silence stretch and sigh,
While the fireflies flutter by,
Nature holds her breath in peace,
In this stillness, joys increase.

Every shadow tells a tale,
Of great journeys, loss, and sail,
Dreamers dance upon the breeze,
In a world that aims to please.

Awake, but still in soft repose,
In the twilight's subtle glow,
Slumbering landscapes, deep and wide,
Invite the wanderers inside.

Beneath the Quiet Canopy

Whispers circle through the trees,
Rustling leaves, a gentle breeze,
Sunlight filters, dimmed and soft,
Nature's embrace, we drift aloft.

Underneath the boughs so green,
Secrets held, seldom seen,
Petrichor after gentle rain,
In this space, no room for pain.

Birds weave songs, a tranquil thread,
Each note held where time is led,
Branches sway in rhythmic grace,
Peaceful moments interlace.

Stars above begin to gleam,
As shadows fall like whispered dream,
Beneath the canopy we find,
The stillness that can bind the mind.

Veils of twilight softly spun,
In nature's cradle, we are one,
Here, where heartbeats sync in tune,
Beneath the watchful silver moon.

Hushed Reflections

Mirrored lake beneath the pines,
Calmly holds the world's designs,
In its depths, a silent song,
Echoes where the still belong.

Pebbles resting, soft and round,
Whispers echo, nature's sound,
Ripples dance where gazes met,
Time stands still, a soft duet.

Morning fog, a tender veil,
Secrets held within the trail,
While the sun, in gold array,
Wakes the world to greet the day.

Reflections alter, slowly shift,
Memories in water drift,
Hushed and quiet, all around,
In this stillness, lost is found.

Each moment, like a breath,
Captures life, escapes from death,
Hushed reflections guide our way,
Through the dawn of a new day.

The Stillness Between Moments

A pause in time, a space to breathe,
Where thoughts can rest and gently weave,
In this hush, the heart stands still,
Listening close to nature's will.

Petals fall without a sound,
In the quiet, peace is found,
Each heartbeat echoes soft and clear,
Moments cherished, ever near.

Dancing shadows, flickers bright,
Create pictures in the night,
Holding time in fragile hands,
Life unfolds in silent strands.

Gathered dreams, like dew at dawn,
Sparkle brightly, then are gone,
Yet the stillness leaves its mark,
Guiding us through light and dark.

In the silence, wisdom sings,
Of all the joy that stillness brings,
The moments breathe, they intertwine,
In the stillness, life aligns.

Whispers of the Soothing Night

In shadows deep, the moonlight glows,
It wraps the world in gentle prose.
A tranquil breeze, soft and slow,
Whispers secrets only night can know.

Stars shimmer bright in velvet blue,
While dreams awaken, fresh and new.
The heart finds peace in night's embrace,
A serene moment, a holy space.

Crickets sing their nightly hymn,
As daylight fades, the chances dim.
In twilight's arms, we find our rest,
In whispered thoughts, we feel the best.

The world slows down; time seems to pause,
In nighttime's grasp, we find our cause.
With each soft sigh, we drift and sway,
In the soothing night, we lose our way.

So close your eyes; let worries cease,
In whispers soft, we find our peace.
The night will guard, the stars will guide,
In soothing silence, we abide.

As Stars Unfurl

In the navy sky, a tale unfolds,
As stars uncoil and bright stories told.
Each twinkle sparkles with insight,
Painting dreams in the depths of night.

A canvas vast, where wishes fly,
On celestial wings, they twine and sigh.
Anonymous hopes, they drift and gleam,
As the universe cradles each dream.

Constellations dance, a timeless art,
Connecting souls, hearts that won't part.
In distant realms, destinies weave,
As stars unroll, we dare to believe.

Night whispers secrets the daylight hides,
In the starlit tapestry, hope abides.
With every shimmer, a chance to start,
Uniting the lost with an open heart.

So gaze above, let wonder unfurl,
In the midnight sky, watch the magic whirl.
For as stars stretch wide, dreams take flight,
In this celestial dance, we find our light.

The Calm After the Storm

When thunder fades and skies grow clear,
The calm descends, the end is near.
Raindrops dance on leaves anew,
A gentle hush, a world in blue.

Birds sing sweetly, their songs of grace,
Nature smiles, in a tender embrace.
The earth breathes deep, a silent sigh,
As peace returns beneath the sky.

Puddles glisten, reflections bright,
A mirrored canvas, nature's light.
Every blade sways, a promise made,
In this stillness, fears will fade.

Sunbeams break through, a golden lace,
Kissing the ground, the flowers' face.
Healing whispers linger in air,
The calm after the storm, beyond compare.

With every dawn, new hope is born,
In the tender light of the morn.
Though storms may visit, they come and go,
In the calm's embrace, our spirits grow.

Embracing the Lull

In twilight's arms, we softly sway,
As day gives way to night's ballet.
The world slows down, a gentle hush,
In this calm moment, feel the rush.

Whispers of dreams begin to rise,
Underneath the tapestry of skies.
Every heartbeat finds its tune,
As shadows dance beneath the moon.

The stars align, a guiding light,
In this serene and quiet night.
With every breath, we drift away,
Embracing the lull, come what may.

Soft melodies float on the breeze,
Wrapped in the night, we find our ease.
A lullaby sung by the night,
Filling our hearts with pure delight.

So hold this moment, let it flow,
In the embrace of the night's soft glow.
For here we find a sacred space,
In the hush of night, we find our place.

Lullaby of Stillness

Whispers dance in twilight's glow,
Softly cradling dreams below.
Stars adorn the velvet night,
Silent echoes, pure delight.

Moonbeams lace the slumbered air,
Tender sighs that linger there.
In this calm, the world will pause,
Nature hums its sweet applause.

Close your eyes, the world is still,
Wrapped in peace, your heart will fill.
Let the gentle night embrace,
Time slips by, a silent grace.

In the hush where dreams reside,
Find your thoughts in evening's tide.
Every heartbeat's soft refrain,
Calls the night to bloom again.

Rest beneath the darkened dome,
In this space, you are at home.
Lullabies of softest sound,
Hold you close, the night unbound.

Dreaming Skies

Clouds drift softly, dreams take flight,
Painted hues in morning light.
Whispers of a world above,
Stitch our hearts with threads of love.

Beneath the vast and twinkling blue,
Every moment feels so new.
Chasing hopes like drifting leaves,
In the heart, a treasure weaves.

Stars will wink with ancient tales,
Guiding ships on silver trails.
Restless shadows, playful breeze,
Invite us to explore with ease.

Sunset flames in golden rows,
Colors fade as daylight goes.
In this dream, we find our way,
Through the night, we'll learn to sway.

Let your spirit freely soar,
In the sky, forevermore.
Every cloud, a dream embraced,
Through the heavens, ever chased.

Gentle Hands of Time

Ticking softly, moments fly,
Fleeting whispers like a sigh.
Gentle hands that shape our day,
Tugging at the heart to stay.

With each tick, the memories blend,
Hoping time will never end.
Soft reminders, sweet and pure,
In our hearts, we find the cure.

Seasons shift, as shadows cast,
Moments cherished, hold them fast.
Time, a river, flowing free,
Guides our souls to harmony.

Every laugh, each tear we share,
Time's embrace, beyond compare.
Softly urging us to grow,
Like the tides that ebb and flow.

Woven threads of joy and pain,
In the dance of sun and rain.
Cherish every heartbeat's chime,
In the gentle hands of time.

The Peaceful Tides

Waves roll softly, kiss the shore,
Whispers of the ocean's lore.
Each tide brings a soothing song,
In their rhythm, hearts belong.

Glistening beneath the sun,
A tranquil place where dreams have spun.
Footprints fade like fleeting thoughts,
In the sands, our souls are caught.

Moonlight weaves through ocean's veil,
Guiding boats with silver trail.
In the stillness, echoes call,
Reminding us to rise and fall.

Seashell treasures, stories share,
Nature's gifts laid out with care.
Embrace the calm, let worries slide,
Find your peace within the tide.

Let the waves embrace your mind,
In their depths, true peace you'll find.
Flowing softly, ever wide,
In the heart, the peaceful tide.

The Quiet Heavens Above

Stars whisper softly, in the dark sky,
A blanket of silence, as the night sighs.
Moonlight dances on dreams intertwined,
In the gentle embrace, our hearts aligned.

Clouds drift like shadows, light on the ground,
Each twinkle a promise, forever unbound.
In the still of the night, our hopes ignite,
Guided by the glow, we embrace the light.

Comets blaze trails, a fleeting delight,
Providing brief solace, in the still of night.
Beneath this vast canvas, we ponder our way,
With love as our compass, we'll never stray.

Galaxies call us, with secrets to share,
In the quiet heavens, we're free as the air.
Time slows to a whisper, our worries set free,
In the vastness above, we're destined to be.

Here in the silence, we find our true selves,
In the quiet heavens, our spirit compels.
Holding hands gently, on this celestial stage,
Our dreams intertwine, as we turn the page.

Emptiness of the Crystal Sea

Waves crash lightly, whispers of grace,
In the crystal sea, we find our place.
Endless horizons, beckoning wide,
With the sun's reflection, our fears collide.

Dropped anchors of sorrow, lost in the depth,
Each ripple a memory, each breath a theft.
Yet in this stillness, we learn to embrace,
Some emptiness holds, a different space.

Seagulls call out, a forgotten song,
Dreams on the water, where we feel strong.
In the flowing tides, we discover our core,
In the emptiness, we yearn for more.

Beneath the surface, a world waits in pause,
The crystal sea listens, without any cause.
In its deep heart lies, untold truths to find,
An ocean of echoes, unbound, intertwined.

And as the sun sets, painting skies anew,
We'll dance with the waves, as stars break through.
In the emptiness, we gather our dreams,
In the crystal sea, life's beauty redeems.

Harmony in Every Breath

Inhale the morning, a song softly sung,
Dancing with petals, where hope has sprung.
Every heartbeat whispers, in rhythms divine,
In the tapestry woven, your soul and mine.

With each step we take, harmony sways,
Nature's chorus beckons, in vibrant displays.
Raindrops like laughter, a symphony clear,
In the arms of stillness, our worries disappear.

Breezes cradle secrets, on the edge of the day,
In every connection, our doubts melt away.
The sun's warm embrace, ignites passions anew,
In every breath shared, I find my way to you.

Moonlight serenades, soft lullabies hum,
Bringing peace to our minds, as shadows succumb.
In the stillness of night, dreams rise and unfold,
Creating a harmony, worth more than gold.

So let's breathe together, in this dance of grace,
Finding joy in the journey, in time and space.
With love as our rhythm, we'll step through the tide,
In harmony's embrace, forever we'll glide.

Silent Horizons

Birds take flight, across the still sky,
Tracing silent paths, where dreams fly high.
The sun dips low, painting shadows just right,
In the quiet of dusk, we find our light.

Mountains stand guard, with secrets to share,
Whispers of nature, float freely in air.
In the twilight glow, horizons extend,
A promise of journeys, where paths will bend.

Waves kiss the shore, in a soft embrace,
Every grain of sand holds a quiet grace.
Together we wander, into the unknown,
Finding peace in silence, love overgrown.

The horizon calls, with a soft, beckoning glow,
Leading our souls where the wild winds blow.
In stillness we stand, hearts open and free,
In silent horizons, just you and me.

As night falls gently, stars twinkle bright,
With every spark lit, our spirits take flight.
In this vastness we trust, as the world spins around,
In silent horizons, true love is found.

Echoes of Calmness

In the hush of twilight's glow,
Whispers travel soft and slow.
Gentle breezes stir the trees,
Nature's sighs, a soothing tease.

Moonlight dances on the stream,
Lost within a tranquil dream.
Stars peek down with watchful eyes,
Guarding peace beneath the skies.

Mountains rise, steadfast and grand,
Embracing all with open hand.
Their silence echoes through the night,
A canvas painted soft and bright.

In stillness, thoughts begin to weave,
Threads of calm, make me believe.
Every heartbeat finds its place,
In this quiet, warm embrace.

As the world slows down its race,
Time suspends with gentle grace.
Echoes of a sweet refrain,
In this stillness, I remain.

A Symphony of Quietude

Softly falling, leaves descend,
Nature's lullaby, a friend.
Silken whispers greet the air,
Moments linger, pure and rare.

Water flows in gentle streams,
Cradling all our simplest dreams.
Beneath the shade of ancient oaks,
Calm surrounds; it gently cloaks.

Birdsong twirls in dawn's first light,
Crickets serenade the night.
Each note blends, a fluid line,
In this symphony, I shine.

Veils of silence draw me near,
Where the soul can shed its fear.
With every breath, I find my tune,
In this space, I am attuned.

Life can rush and pull away,
Yet here, peace will always stay.
A symphony of heartbeats flows,
In quietude, true beauty grows.

Hidden Sanctuaries

In the forest, secrets hide,
Paths where countless dreams reside.
Mossy stones, the whispers call,
In hidden places, I can sprawl.

A gentle brook wraps round the trees,
Carrying tales upon the breeze.
Dappled sunlight warms my face,
Here, I find my sacred space.

Amidst the thicket, shadows play,
Nature's charm, a soft ballet.
Each step taken is a song,
In these woods, I belong.

Moments frozen, time stands still,
Every heartbeat, slow and chill.
Tucked away from the world's race,
Hidden sanctuaries embrace.

Leaves converse in rustling tones,
This is where my spirit roams.
In solitude, I find the light,
Hidden sanctuaries ignite.

Time Paused

Here within the shaded glen,
Moments stretch and repeat again.
Gentle stillness fills my mind,
In this pause, true peace I find.

Clouds drift by in skies so blue,
Painting dreams with every hue.
Thoughts like feathers float away,
In this quiet, they can stay.

Every breath a whispered prayer,
Suspended here, without a care.
Time unfolds in soft embrace,
Every heartbeat finds its pace.

Memories linger, gently spun,
As daylight fades, the shadows run.
In twilight's grip, I feel so free,
Time paused, just the world and me.

Underneath the canopy,
Life slows down and sings with glee.
In this moment, beauty shows,
Time paused, and serenity grows.

Veil of Serenity

Soft whispers of the night,
Stars twinkle, hearts take flight.
In shadows, calmness we find,
Gentle breezes blow, unkind.

A tranquil world, no sound profound,
Embraced by silence all around.
In the stillness, dreams can bloom,
Cradled in the evening's gloom.

Waves of peace wash over me,
In the dark, I feel so free.
A veil of stars above my head,
Through the night, my spirit's led.

Beneath the moon, I softly tread,
Soft is the path where once I fled.
With every breath, the night unfolds,
A story of the quiet told.

In this place where time surrenders,
Each moment, a gift that lingers.
Wrapped in night's sweet embrace,
I find my heart, my sacred space.

The Solitary Path

Walking down this quiet road,
Step by step, I bear my load.
Loneliness, my only friend,
With each stride, the thoughts descend.

The trees whisper secrets low,
A hidden world, where no one goes.
Footprints fade in evening's glow,
A journey only I can know.

Clouds drift softly overhead,
In solitude, I lay my head.
Each echo sings of paths unseen,
In silence, I can find the keen.

Time moves slow, yet I am fast,
In the present, hold the past.
Each breath is like a quiet tune,
Serenading me 'neath the moon.

Here within this lonesome space,
I find my peace, my own embrace.
On this path I choose to roam,
In solitude, I am at home.

Peaceful Resurgence

Amidst the chaos, I retreat,
In silence, feel my heart's soft beat.
Renewed by nature, fresh and bright,
A gentle spark ignites the night.

The rivers flow, a soothing sound,
In their rhythm, hope is found.
With every drop, my worries fade,
In this peace, I am remade.

Sunrise paints the dawn anew,
Colors dance in vibrant hue.
From ashes risen, I will soar,
In this moment, I'll restore.

The whispers of the morning breeze,
Caress my soul, bring me to ease.
In every leaf, in every tree,
Life blooms again, inviting me.

From shadows deep, I break away,
Reclaim my strength, embrace the day.
With grateful heart, I rise and sing,
In this resurgence, joy takes wing.

A Haven of Quiet

In corners dim, where shadows play,
A sanctuary, night and day.
Cradled close in gentle arms,
Where silence weaves its soothing charms.

The clock ticks slow, time stands still,
In this space, my heart will fill.
A haven carved from tranquil air,
Wrapped in peace beyond compare.

Soft candles glow, their flickers dance,
Illuminating dreams of chance.
With every breath, I feel secure,
In solitude, my spirit pure.

Here the world fades far away,
In quietude, I long to stay.
Whispers linger, soft and low,
In this haven, I find my flow.

So let me rest, my worries cease,
In this calm, I find my peace.
A haven built on love and light,
A sanctuary, my heart's delight.

Chasing Moonlight

Under the silver glow of night,
Two hearts wander, took flight.
Dreams dance in the cool breeze,
Whispers linger among the trees.

Stars twinkle in velvet skies,
Hope reflected in our eyes.
Each step leads a secret path,
Caught in the moon's gentle wrath.

Shadows stretch, the world asleep,
In this magic, memories we keep.
Hand in hand, we chase the dream,
Together in this silver beam.

Laughter echoes through the night,
Crafting joy, pure and bright.
The moonlight, our guiding star,
Show us who we truly are.

As dawn approaches, whispers fade,
In our hearts, the promise stayed.
A journey written in the light,
Chasing dreams until daylight.

A Shelter of Solitude

In quiet corners, shadows grow,
Where the softest secrets flow.
Whispers of the soul arise,
Beneath the vast and open skies.

Time slows in this sacred space,
Finding peace, a gentle grace.
The world outside can wait a while,
In solitude, I find my smile.

Nature sings a tender tune,
Bathe me in the warmest June.
Leaves rustle, a calming sigh,
Underneath the watchful sky.

With every breath, I feel alive,
In solitude, my spirit thrives.
A shelter built from whispered thoughts,
In quietness, blissfully sought.

The heart unwinds, a gentle thread,
In tranquil moments, fears are shed.
Here, I bloom, an endless quest,
In this haven, find my rest.

The Soft Hour

As sunlight dips, the world turns gold,
A softer hour, stories unfold.
Shadows lengthen, skies ablaze,
In this moment, I lose my gaze.

Warmth envelops the gentle scene,
Where hues of love and calm convene.
Time slows down, a fleeting sigh,
In this soft hour, I learn to fly.

Birds sing sweetly, the day departs,
Painting with whispers, soothing hearts.
A canvas filled with fleeting light,
Weaving dreams into the night.

Stars awaken, blinking bright,
Kindling hopes in the fading light.
A lullaby for weary souls,
In this soft hour, the magic rolls.

Embrace the dusk, let go the race,
In gentle stillness, find your place.
As darkness falls, beauty stays,
In this soft hour, love displays.

Portraits of Peace

In quiet moments, peace appears,
Painting portraits, calming fears.
Left in silence, a gentle hand,
Crafting solace, subtle and grand.

Through open fields and flowing streams,
Nature weaves the softest dreams.
A breeze carries the whispered sound,
Of joy and love that knows no bound.

In the stillness, shadows melt,
In every heartbeat, kindness felt.
Fragments of laughter fill the air,
Brushing souls with utmost care.

Eyes meet softly, a knowing glance,
In shared stillness, we find our dance.
Connections rooted, deep and wide,
In this portrait, peace abides.

Every hue tells a story true,
From heart to heart, breaking through.
With each stroke, a promise stays,
In portraits of peace, love displays.

Twilight's Caress

Soft shadows creep, the day does fade,
Colors mingle, a serenade.
Whispers linger, the night is near,
Wrapped in silence, the stars appear.

Gentle breezes dance and sway,
Nature rests at end of day.
Moonlight spills on dewy grass,
Time stands still as moments pass.

Crickets sing their evening tune,
While fireflies light up the gloom.
A canvas brushed with hues of gold,
In twilight's arms, our dreams unfold.

Time's embrace, a soothing balm,
In this hour, the world feels calm.
With every breath, we let love flow,
In twilight's caress, hearts aglow.

As night descends, the magic grows,
In silence, the universe knows.
So let us linger, hand in hand,
In twilight's caress, we shall stand.

Still Waters Run Deep

Still waters lie beneath the trees,
Reflecting skies and gentle breeze.
A quiet peace envelops all,
Where nature's whispers softly call.

Ripples dance on the surface clear,
Echoes of moments held so dear.
In solitude, the heart finds grace,
In stillness, we embrace our space.

Depths untold beneath the calm,
In silence there is hidden charm.
The mirrored world holds secrets tight,
Yet stirs the soul to take its flight.

As thoughts drift like leaves in the air,
A tranquil heart can lay its care.
For still waters, with tranquil gleam,
Reflect the hush of a waking dream.

In this embrace, we find our way,
Guided by shadows that gently play.
Still waters run deep, listen close,
For in this stillness, we find repose.

A Symphony of Silence

In the hush, our secrets lie,
Where words dare not to wander by.
A symphony plays in muted tones,
In silence, the heart finds its own.

Soft sighs hover, the air stands still,
Each moment ripe, an unspoken thrill.
Beneath the calm, a heartbeats sound,
In quietude, our souls are found.

Gentle echoes sweep the night,
In solitude, we feel the light.
The world breathes deep in this embrace,
In silence, we discover grace.

A dance of shadows, a tender weave,
In every pause, we learn to believe.
In every sigh, a story unfolds,
In the symphony, the silence holds.

So let us sit in this sacred space,
For in stillness, we know our place.
A symphony built on whispers sweet,
In silence, our hearts shall meet.

The Last Light of Day

The sun dips low, a golden ray,
Embracing night, it bids goodbye.
Colors fade in a soft display,
As shadows stretch across the sky.

The horizon blushes, kissed by fire,
Painting dreams that never tire.
In the twilight's gentle glow,
We find the peace that we all know.

Birds call home as daylight wanes,
In silent flight, they break their chains.
A moment held, a breath that's shared,
In the magic of dusk laid bare.

Stars awaken, one by one,
The night's embrace has just begun.
Yet in this hour, hearts are light,
In the dance between day and night.

So let us cherish the fading light,
For in its warmth, all feels right.
The last light of day softly fades,
In memories kept, love never wanes.

Time's Gentle Suspension

Moments linger, soft and slow,
Whispers of the past we know.
The clock sighs with a tender grace,
In stillness, we embrace this space.

Dreams unfold like petals wide,
In golden hues, they bloom inside.
Each second flows, a gentle stream,
Caught between a thought and dream.

Memories dance on twilight's edge,
Beyond the limits of a pledge.
In quietude, we find our way,
Lost in the promise of today.

Hearts beat softly, bonds renew,
Infinite skies painted in blue.
We sip the stillness like fine wine,
In this moment, we intertwine.

A breath held tight, the world fades out,
Inside this pause, we toss about.
Time's gentle hands, they cradle us,
In this silence, we find trust.

Embracing the Twilight

The sky drapes in a dusky hue,
A blend of gold and shades of blue.
Stars peek out from their hiding place,
Night invites us with a warm embrace.

Shadows stretch like arms so wide,
Welcoming dreams with nowhere to hide.
The moon whispers secrets of the night,
Guiding lost souls toward the light.

Crickets sing their evening song,
In nature's chorus, we belong.
As dark descends, we shed our day,
Wrapped in twilight's soft ballet.

Time stands still in this lovely scene,
Every corner feels serene.
In twilight's glow, hearts beat as one,
A gentle dance until we're done.

With each breath, we pull the night,
Embracing dreams in soft twilight.
Here in silence, we can learn,
That in the dusk, our spirits burn.

Soothing Shadows

Underneath a velvet sky,
Shadows flicker, softly sigh.
Each silhouette holds a tale,
In their embrace, we shall prevail.

Moonlight dances on the ground,
In whispered secrets, peace is found.
Gentle breezes caress our skin,
Inviting solace from within.

As darkness wraps the world in care,
We find our strength, we start to share.
In solitude, we learn to heal,
Every heartbeat becomes real.

The night unfolds like a warm quilt,
We gather dreams, though once we spilt.
In soothing shadows, fears are cast,
Whispers of hope, from first to last.

Wandering softly through the dark,
Every moment leaves a mark.
In quietude, we find our song,
As shadows linger, we belong.

A Canvas of Calm

Painted skies in gentle paint,
Brushes whisper, colors faint.
Each stroke carries a soothing balm,
Creating spaces warm and calm.

The canvas breathes, a silent sigh,
Soft hues merge, as day waves goodbye.
Pastels glow, with an artist's touch,
In this peace, we feel so much.

Textures mingle, soft and light,
Holding secrets of the night.
In every corner, dreams arise,
A world reborn beneath the skies.

Layers deepen, stories unfold,
Timeless tales, both new and old.
With gentle whispers painted bright,
We find ourselves in the twilight.

The palette swirls with hues of grace,
In calm, our hearts find their place.
A canvas stretched beyond the seam,
Where life and art blend into dream.

The Lullabies of Nature

In the whispering trees, soft shadows play,
As moonlight dances, greeting the day.
Birds sing sweetly, a gentle refrain,
Nature's lullabies wash away all pain.

The rivers hum quietly, a soothing stream,
Crickets join in, weaving a dream.
The stars twinkle softly, a diamond-studded sky,
In the arms of the night, we tenderly sigh.

Winds carry secrets through meadows wide,
While flowers nod gently, the garden's pride.
Each petal a note in this symphony,
Nature's soft serenade, pure harmony.

The mountains stand tall, guardians of time,
Their echoes resonate, a metered chime.
Rest now, dear child, let worries take flight,
For the lullabies of nature cradle the night.

In this tranquil world, peace reigns supreme,
Embrace the stillness, drift into a dream.
For tomorrow will come, with its song to unfold,
But tonight, let nature's beauty enfold.

Crickets' Night Songs

When twilight descends, the world is still,
Crickets begin their serenade, a thrill.
Chirping softly, in rhythm they play,
With each note, they chase twilight away.

In fields of green, their chorus ignites,
A melody woven through starry nights.
The moon smiles down, an audience bless,
As crickets perform in the night's soft dress.

With every chirp, a story is told,
Of warmth and of peace, of dreams to unfold.
Their song is a beacon, a guide through the dark,
Illuminating paths where the soft shadows park.

Their symphony swells, in the still summer air,
A magical rhythm that banishes fear.
Each note a reminder, life's pulse is strong,
In the chorus of crickets, we all belong.

As night deepens, their voices remain,
A tapestry woven, from joy and from pain.
For as long as we listen, in calm or in strife,
Crickets will sing of the beauty in life.

Still Waters Run Deep

The lake lies serene, a mirror of night,
Reflecting soft stars, a tranquil sight.
Beneath its calm surface, secrets reside,
In still waters run deep, where mysteries hide.

Ripples break gently, a splash of delight,
The moon casts its glow, bathing all in light.
Whispers of breezes, through tall willows weave,
In the heart of the quiet, we learn how to believe.

On the edge of the shore, dreams come alive,
In the depths of our souls, hopes bravely thrive.
Each moment a treasure, so simple, so sweet,
In the stillness of waters, our journeys repeat.

Reflections of life dance upon the pond,
Echoes of laughter, of silence, of bond.
The stillness speaks volumes, if only we hear,
In still waters run deep, there's nothing to fear.

Let us gather our thoughts, like leaves in a stream,
Flowing softly together, united in dream.
For in the calm dark, we discover our quest,
In still waters run deep, we find our true rest.

Light at the End of the Dusk

As the sun dips low, hues of gold embrace,
A soft sigh of evening, darkness to face.
But amid the shadows, a flicker shines bright,
A promise of dawn, in the heart of the night.

The stars twinkle gently, a glimmer of grace,
In the canvas of twilight, dreams find their place.
Each moment a heartbeat, each breath a new start,
For light at the end is a hope in our heart.

The horizon whispers, as night slowly creeps,
Of journeys uncharted, where the spirit leaps.
With every soft shadow, new paths are revealed,
For light at the end, our fears are repealed.

Embrace the darkness, let it unfold,
Within its soft cocoon, let courage take hold.
As twilight surrenders, and shadows depart,
The light at the end shines bright in our heart.

So when the dusk settles, and silence draws near,
Remember the light, for it's always here.
In the dance of the stars, in the whispers of night,
There's always a beacon, a guiding light.

Milton Keynes UK
Ingram Content Group UK Ltd.
UKHW010230111224
452348UK00011B/635